WJEC
CBAC

KW-554-089

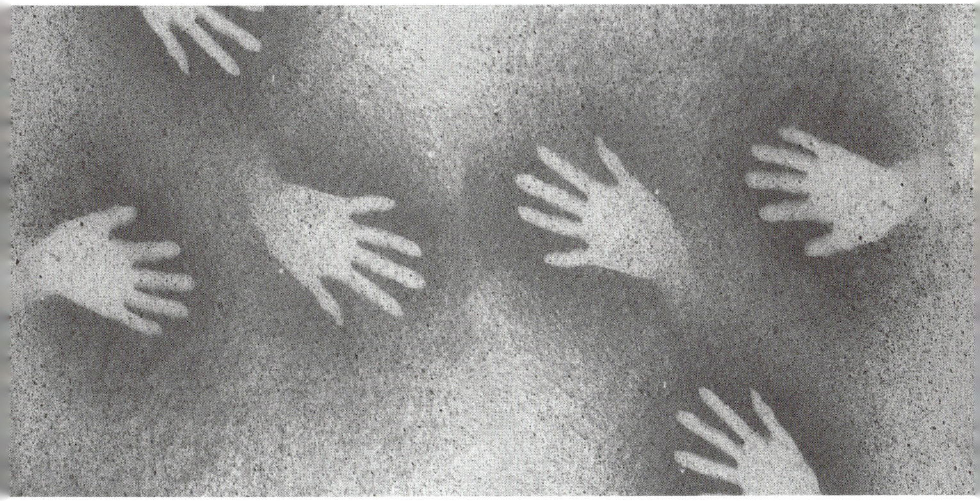

WJEC GCSE ENGLISH LITERATURE

SKILLS AND PRACTICE

STEVEN CROFT

Consultant:
Roger Lane

OXFORD
UNIVERSITY PRESS

OxBox

Contents

Contents

Preparing for Assessment

To do well in your English Literature GCSE you need to understand what each element of your course involves so that you can prepare for it carefully. Your GCSE is divided into four units:

Unit 1: Different Cultures Prose and Contemporary Poetry. This unit is worth 35% of your final mark and is tested by a written exam lasting 2 hours.

Unit 2: Either Literary Heritage Drama and Contemporary Prose (2a) or Contemporary Drama and Literary Heritage Prose (2b). This unit is worth 40% of your final mark and is tested by a written exam lasting 2 hours.

Unit 3: Literary Heritage Poetry and Drama. This unit is worth 25% of your final mark and is tested by Controlled Assessment.

Preparing for the written exams

The written exams make up 75% of your total marks for GCSE.

1. Planning and preparing

Careful planning and preparation is essential if you are to be successful in your exams. Some of this preparation will take place throughout the course and some of it in the weeks immediately before you take your exams.

Throughout the course

- Be prepared to read your set texts. Don't attempt this all in one go. Be systematic, such as reading a chapter per week.
- Wider reading will help you improve your vocabulary, understanding of sentence structures and knowledge of how texts of different kinds are written and organized.
- When you read different kinds of texts, think carefully about how writers use language in different ways to create particular effects.

Planning your revision

- Begin your revision in good time.
- Organize your revision carefully and put together a revision timetable to make sure that you can cover all the material you wish to cover in the time available.
- Make sure that you know exactly what to expect on each of your exam papers. Look at past papers and at the sample questions in this book (as well as in your Student Book). Practise answering these questions in the same amount of time that you will have available in the real exam.
- Look at the mark schemes for your exam papers – these will show you what the examiners are looking for. (Ask your teacher about them or you can find them on the examination board's website.)

2. The question paper

You can save yourself a lot of time by making yourself aware of what to expect on each question paper. This is something that you can do **before** the exam, by looking at past exam papers. You can also find key information about each exam paper in the **Exam insight** section at the start of each unit in this book.

This tells you the name of the unit you are covering and the level. Make sure you have the correct paper before you begin.

This tells you the amount of time you have to complete the exam.

This lists any other materials you will receive alongside the exam booklet.

Read these instructions carefully <u>before</u> you begin answering, and follow them exactly.

You should also read this additional information closely before you begin.

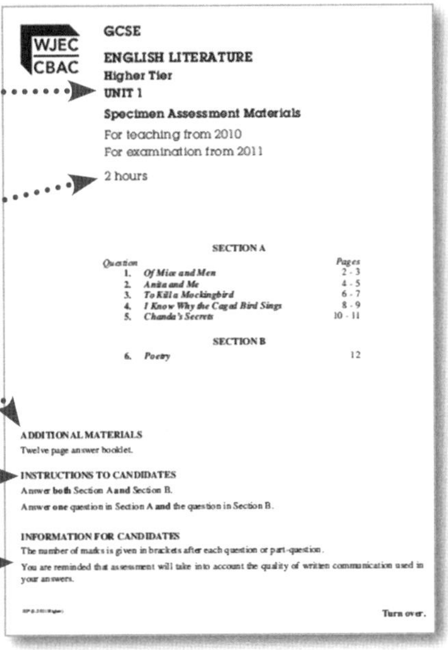
WJEC CBAC

GCSE
ENGLISH LITERATURE
Higher Tier
UNIT 1
Specimen Assessment Materials
For teaching from 2010
For examination from 2011

2 hours

SECTION A

Question		Pages
1.	*Of Mice and Men*	2 - 3
2.	*Anita and Me*	4 - 5
3.	*To Kill a Mockingbird*	6 - 7
4.	*I Know Why the Caged Bird Sings*	8 - 9
5.	*Chanda's Secrets*	10 - 11

SECTION B

6.	*Poetry*	12

ADDITIONAL MATERIALS
Twelve page answer booklet.

INSTRUCTIONS TO CANDIDATES
Answer **both** Section A **and** Section B.
Answer **one** question in Section A **and** the question in Section B.

INFORMATION FOR CANDIDATES
The number of marks is given in brackets after each question or part-question.
You are reminded that assessment will take into account the quality of written communication used in your answers.

Turn over.

3. Planning and checking your answers

- Read the questions with a pen in your hand and underline key words.
- If the question includes an extract, make sure that you read it to the end. Try to read it with the wording of the question in mind and underline or circle important phrases.
- Be aware of how much time you have available for each question and use this time effectively.
- Make sure that you leave yourself a few minutes at the end of the exam to check your spelling, punctuation, grammar and paragraphing.

4. Aiming for A*

To achieve a top grade you must be able to:

- structure your answer effectively and write clearly and fluently
- use accurate spelling, punctuation and grammar
- show that you have an overview of each text and the ability to move from more general ideas to specific points
- convey your ideas persuasively and coherently using relevant evidence from the texts to support your points.

Preparing for unseen texts

In Unit 1 Section B you will answer questions on two unseen contemporary poems.

What does 'unseen' mean?

The poems you will be given on the exam paper for Unit 1 are likely to be:

- poems that you have never seen before
- poems that you have not studied as part of your course.

This is what is meant by 'unseen' texts.

The exam question will test your ability to:

- respond to the poems, examining the themes, issues and ideas that the poems explore
- analyse the techniques that the poets use and explore the effects
- compare the two poems in terms of ideas, techniques and style.

Revising for 'unseen' poems

Unlike other parts of your GCSE English Literature assessment there are no specific texts to be studied or revised for this exam and you therefore need to adopt a different approach to preparing for this part of your course.

Here are some things you can do:

- read a range of different kinds of poems such as those used on past papers
- identify the kinds of things that you can look for and comment on in poems
- as you read poems throughout your course, make brief notes on:
  - the ideas and themes explored
  - the use of various poetic techniques to achieve effects
- practise writing about poetry – try to develop a structured and organized approach
- practise making sensible comparisons.

Writing about linked texts

For Unit 3 you will need to produce an assignment under controlled conditions in which you link literary heritage poetry to a Shakespeare text. The focus of you assessment will be to show that you understand your texts and that you can carry out a close study of the language and techniques used by each writer.

In order to prepare yourself for this assignment you will need to:

- be able to make meaningful comments about the writer's use of language
- have a detailed understanding of your Shakespeare play, particularly how it ends and how characters in the play change as the play progresses
- have a detailed understanding of the poems that you are focusing on
- be able to respond personally to the poems and the Shakespeare text you have sudied
- when you write your response, you should be able to write about at least two poems in detail and have an overall sense of the other poems
- when you write about your Shakespeare text, you may choose to focus on one or two scenes in detail but you should also have a clear understanding of the whole play
- identify how your Shakespeare and poetry texts are linked
- explore these links and show what they reveal about the texts overall.

Preparing for Controlled Assessment

What is Controlled Assessment?

Controlled Assessment is a way of assessing your work in a controlled situation, which is not a formal exam. As in an exam, Controlled Assessment tasks are set by the exam board but your work will be marked by your teacher. You will be allowed to prepare for your assignment in class and discuss the task with other students. However, you must complete the final piece of work independently.

The stages of Controlled Assessment

Controlled Assessment takes place in three stages:

introduction to the task → research and preparation (limited supervision) → writing the assignment (formal supervision)

Introduction to the task

Your teacher will introduce you to the task and make sure that you know what to do and what is required of you.

Research and preparation

During this part of the process you will be able to work under 'limited supervision', which means that you will be able to work without being directly supervised. You may be able to work with other students and some of your work may be done outside the classroom.

Writing your assignment

This is where you write and submit your final piece of work for assessment. You may be asked to complete your assignment in one session or your writing time may be split over more than one session. This stage will be completed under 'formal supervision', which means you will be supervised at all times and will not be allowed to use reference materials or discuss your work with other students.

1. Preparing the task

Once your teacher has introduced the task you will spend some time preparing for your Controlled Assessment. During this time your teacher will be able to discuss the task with you but will only be allowed to give you general advice.

During this stage of the assessment you should:

- work out how you are going to approach the task
- think about your task and develop your ideas
- organize and structure your ideas.

2. Writing your response

You will write your assessment under formal supervision. Remember to:

- do everything the task asks you to do
- write in Standard English using full sentences and paragraphs – do not write in note form
- keep track of the time available and leave yourself enough time at the end to read through and check your work.

3. Checking your work

Make sure that you read your work before handing it in. You should check that:

- you have not made any errors in spelling or punctuation
- you have used sentences and paragraphs correctly
- you have not made any grammatical mistakes.

4. Aiming for A*

To achieve a top grade in your assessment, you must be able to:

- show that you have a clear understanding of the demands of the task
- show that you have an overview of the texts you are focusing on
- structure your answer effectively and write clearly and fluently
- write technically accurate English in terms of grammar, punctuation and spelling
- use effective, well-chosen vocabulary
- convey your ideas coherently and persuasively using evidence from the texts to support your ideas.

Key skills

Technical errors in your writing can cost you precious marks and might prevent you achieving a grade C or above. During your course you need to do all you can to improve the standard of your written English. You can do this by:

- being aware of the kind of mistakes you make
- making a note of any particular words you spell incorrectly or punctuation marks you have problems with
- working on the areas you know cause you problems
- checking your work through carefully.

Technical errors usually fall into three main categories:

1. spelling
2. punctuation
3. grammar.

This section outlines some common problem areas to help you revise the basic skills necessary for success at GCSE.

1. Spelling

If you have some difficulties with spelling it does not mean that you will not pass your GCSE but it could hold you back from achieving high marks.

Here are some things you can do to improve your skills.

- Read as much as possible – seeing words in print can help you visualize them as you write.
- Identify words that you frequently spell incorrectly and make a list of them.
- Work at learning the words you struggle with.
- Get into the habit of reading through your written work and checking it for mistakes.

Look at the three lists of commonly misspelt words on the next page and see if you can identify what is wrong with each word.

Then, write down the correct spelling of each one. If you do not know what the word means, look it up in a dictionary and write the meaning down next to the correct spelling.

begining | sentance | metaphores
writter | affective | caracters
similie | comparisen | stansa
rythm | ryme | arguement
auther | oposite | parralel
diference | coloquial | monolog
conotation | narative | speach

Begin a spelling list of your own for words that you sometimes spell incorrectly and watch out for these words in your own writing.

Commonly confused words

Some spelling mistakes happen because one word has been confused with a similar word. Here are some words that are commonly confused:

being – been

- *The characters were being violent to one another.*
- *He had been unable to get help.*

know – now – no

- *I know the writer probably intended this.*
- *Now we see the main character alone.*
- *He had no idea what was going to happen.*

where – wear – were

- *Meena isn't sure where she is.*
- *Lennie wanted to wear his hat like George.*
- *They were looking forward to better times.*

loose – lose

- *The description is quite loose.*
- *He decides he is willing to lose everything.*

The list below includes more words that are often confused. Make sure you know what each one means and when to use it. Try writing a sentence of your own for each word.

affect/effect
accept/except
all ready/already
seen/scene
practise/practice
sight/site
write/right
past/passed
principle/principal

2. Punctuation

Like spelling, correct punctuation is important if you are to achieve the grade you are capable of. Be aware of any particular kinds of punctuation that you have problems with and work on improving your skills.

Here are some key punctuation marks that you should make sure you use accurately in your writing:

- full stops
- question marks
- apostrophes
- speech marks.

Full stops

How you divide your writing up into sentences depends to some extent on what you are writing about and the effects you want to achieve. However, remember that all sentences should make sense as standalone units. Another common mistake is to string together completed statements with commas instead of using full stops to separate them.

Question marks

You will probably be quite clear about where to use question marks but the main problems students have is remembering to put them in – particularly when writing under pressure. Remember:

- do not put a full stop and a question mark together
- do not use a question mark in a sentence that is an indirect question.

Look at the two sentences below. One of them is an example of a direct question and the other an indirect question.

1. ***What is the meaning of the last line***
2. ***The last line makes me question what the meaning could be***

Which sentence do you think needs a question mark?

Apostrophes

Apostrophes are used for two main reasons.

1. They can be used to show where letters have been missed out in shortening words or running two words together (these are called 'contractions'), e.g. *you are – you're; we had – we'd.*
2. They can be used to show that something belongs to someone or something (these are possessive apostrophes). Watch out especially for **its** and **it's**: here 'it's' is a contraction of 'it is', while 'its' is a possessive form indicating something belonging to 'it', e.g. The dog ate <u>its</u> food.

Speech marks

Bear in mind the points below when using speech marks:

- only put the speech marks around the words actually spoken (not the part that tells you who is speaking)
- other punctuation marks relating to what is actually said, such as question marks, exclamation marks, go inside the speech marks
- when two or more people are speaking, remember to start a new line each time a different person speaks.

3. Grammar

Grammatical errors can make your work harder to read and your meaning less clear. Always check your written work through carefully for grammatical mistakes.

The section below details two common mistakes.

Changing tense

Inconsistency in the use of tense can sometimes cause problems for students. Sometimes tenses are incorrectly switched within a paragraph or sometimes even within a sentence.

For example:
Lennie crushed Curley's hand without knowing it. He's shocked by what happens.

Lennie crushed Curley's hand without knowing it: This is written in the past tense but the next sentence – *He's shocked by what happens* – is written in the present tense. The two tenses should agree.

The correct version should read:
Lennie <u>crushes</u> Curley's hand without knowing it. He's shocked by what happens.

Always check your work to make sure that your tenses agree.

Could of, would of, should of

The muddling of 'of' with 'have' is another common mistake because of the similarity in the way the words sound. The correct way of writing these phrases is *could <u>have</u>, would <u>have</u>, should <u>have</u>*. For example: *Scrooge would <u>have</u> continued to act selfishly if he hadn't met the ghosts.*

Unit 1: Different Cultures Prose and Contemporary Poetry

Exam insight

Unit Summary

This unit is assessed by an exam lasting **2 hours**. The exam is worth 35% of your overall marks for this GCSE. The unit is divided into two sections:

Section A: Individual texts in context

Different cultures prose (1 hour recommended).

Section B: Comparative study

Contemporary unseen poetry comparison (1 hour recommended).

Section A: Individual texts in contexts (21%)

For this question you will need to study a prose text from a different culture. You will need to answer **two** questions on your text.

The first question, **part (a)**, will require close reading of an extract that will be printed on the exam paper. It is recommended that you spend 20 minutes on this.

The second question will offer you a choice of two tasks, **parts (b) and (c)**. These questions will relate to the text as a whole and you should only answer **one** of them. You are advised to spend 40 minutes on this part of your exam.

You are not allowed to take copies of your set texts into the exam with you.

Section B: Comparative study (14%)

This section will involve you reading, exploring and responding to two contemporary unseen poems. You should spend 1 hour on this part of your exam. Read the poems with a pen in your hand and make relevant selections from them to answer the question. Look at how the poems are similar and how they are different.

Assessment Objectives

Questions on different cultures prose

For Section A of Unit 1 you will answer two questions on a different cultures prose text. Both questions will test you according to the following Assessment Objectives:

AO1

Respond to the text critically and imaginatively; select and evaluate relevant textual detail to illustrate and support interpretations.

This means that you will need to show in your answer that you have read the text carefully and are able to comment on aspects such as **characters**, **relationships**, **attitudes** and **motives**. You will need to use **well-selected details** from the text to illustrate and support your **ideas**.

The first question, (part (a)), will also test your ability to:

AO2

Explain how language, structure and form contribute to the writer's presentations of ideas, themes and settings.

This means that you will look at the different ways that the writer **uses language to achieve effects** and comment on stylistic features.

The second question, (part (b) or part (c)) will test AO1 and AO4 but **not** AO2. AO4 tests your ability to:

AO4

Relate the text to its social, cultural and historical context; explain how the text has been influential and significant to yourself and other readers in different contexts and at different times.

This means that you will examine how different factors, such as the **historical period**, **social** and **cultural factors** can have an influence on the way a text is written and how it affects the reader.

Question on contemporary poetry

For Section B of Unit 1, you will answer one question comparing contemporary poems. These poems will be 'unseen', which means you will not know what they will be until the day of the exam. For this question, you will be assessed on how well you demonstrate the following skills:

AO1

Respond to the texts critically and imaginatively; select and evaluate relevant textual detail to illustrate and support interpretations.

This means that you need to **read both poems closely**, and show in your answer that you are able to comment on details such as the ideas covered in the poems, **how each poet deals with his or her subject matter** and **how each poet creates mood and atmosphere**. You will need to support your points by selecting and commenting on **relevant quotations** from the texts.

AO2

Explain how language, structure and form contribute to the writers' presentations of ideas, themes and settings.

This means that you will consider **how the writers use language** and **how they structure their poems to** create **particular effects** on the reader. You will also write about stylistic features and what these add to the meaning or impact of each poem.

AO3

Make comparisons and explain links between texts, evaluating writers' different ways of expressing meaning and achieving effects.

This means that you will **compare** the ways in which writers **use language and different techniques** to **express meaning and create effects**. You will make **links** between the poems and identify similarities and differences.

Different cultures prose

Approaching your text

The term 'different cultures prose' is a very broad one and refers to all kinds of prose texts from various parts of the world including the UK.

For this unit you will study one of the following texts:

Of Mice and Men by John Steinbeck
Anita and Me by Meera Syall
To Kill a Mockingbird by Harper Lee
I Know Why the Caged Bird Sings by Maya Angelou
Chandra's Secrets by Allan Stratton.

The prose text that you study for this unit will have much in common with other prose texts that you have studied. However, you might find that it:

- is set in a context that is different from one that you might be familiar with
- presents different lifestyles and ideas
- presents different values or ways of life
- uses non-standard English or dialect forms to reflect the cultural background it focuses on.

Understanding the plot and storyline

Whatever kind of prose text you are studying, the first thing you must do is to read your text in order to get a clear idea of the plot or storyline.

Here are some things you can do to help you develop an overall understanding of your text.

1. Read through the text from beginning to end to get a full sense of the plot. Make sure you know how the book ends and that you have a sense of why the author chose to end it this way.
2. Write a brief summary of the key events of the plot and any important twists and turns.

Make notes on the points below as you study your text.

1. **What is the narrative viewpoint? Is the story told from a first- or third- person perspective?**
2. **Who are the characters? How do they relate to each other? What do they do in the story and how does the writer present them?**
3. **How does the writer use language to present characters and describe settings and to create particular effects?**

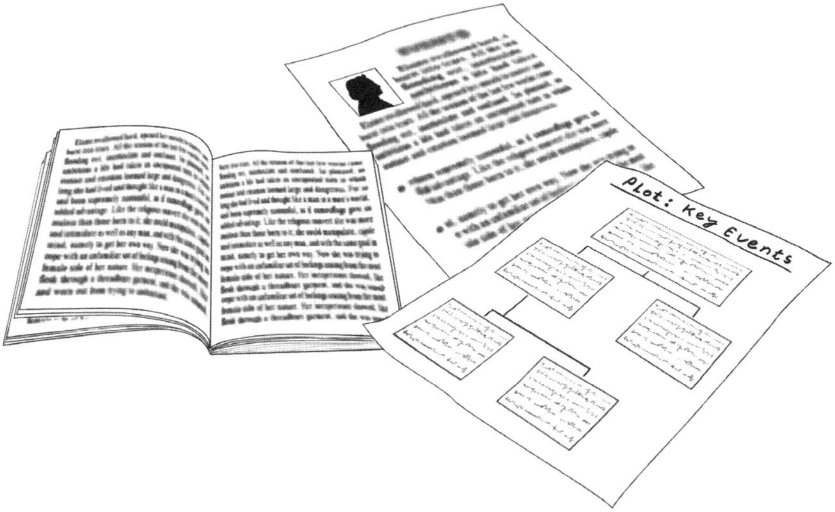

Close reading: analysing characters

Characters are a major part of any novel and writers use a variety of techniques to present them to the reader. It is important that writers create characters that, as readers, we find convincing and believable but you should always think of them as literary creations rather than real people.

The list below suggests some of the ways that writers can present their characters.

- **Description** – writers can tell you what the characters look like, how they are dressed, how they walk and how they talk. They can also describe their physical characteristics. When looking at the writer's description of a character, pay close attention to specific language choices.
- **Speech** – writers often use speech to reveal important information about characters. Look not only at what the characters say but also how they say it. What other characters say about a particular character can also be important.
- **Actions and behaviour** – how characters behave can help to build up a picture of them. Pay attention also to how characters relate to and behave towards other characters.
- **Thoughts and feelings** – narrators often tell you what characters are thinking and feeling.

Look at how the writer presents characters in the extract, below, from *Of Mice and Men* by John Steinbeck.

The first man was small and quick, dark of face, with restless eyes and sharp, strong features. Every part of him was defined: small, strong hands, slender arms, a thin and bony nose. Behind him walked his opposite, a huge man, shapeless of face, with large, pale eyes, with wide, sloping shoulders; and he walked heavily, dragging his feel a little, the way a bear drags his paws. His arms did not swing at his sides, but hung loosely.

The first man stopped short in the clearing, and the follower nearly ran over him. He took off his hat and wiped the sweat-band with his forefinger and snapped the moisture off. His huge companion dropped his blankets and flung himself down and drank from the surface of the green pool; drank with long gulps, snorting into the water like a horse. The small man stepped nervously beside him.

"Lennie!" he said sharply. "Lennie, for God' sakes don't drink so much." Lennie continued to snort into the pool. The small man leaned over and shook him by the shoulder. "Lennie. You gonna be sick like you was last night."

Lennie dipped his whole head under, hat and all, and then he sat up on the bank and his hat dripped down on his blue coat and ran down his back. "Tha's good," he said. "You drink some, George. You take a good big drink." He smiled happily.

George unslung his bindle and dropped it gently on the bank. "I ain't sure it's good water," he said. "Looks kinda scummy."

Lennie dabbled his big paw in the water and wiggled his fingers so the water arose in little splashes; rings widened across the pool to the other side and came back again. Lennie watched them go. "Look, George. Look what I done."

From the extract above what impression do you form of:

a. George

b. Lennie?

Look closely at:

- **how Steinbeck uses language to describe each character**
- **how each character behaves**
- **how the characters respond to each other**
- **what the characters say and how they say it.**

Use specific examples from the extract to illustrate your points.

Close reading: setting and context

The setting and context of a novel is important for several reasons:

- it forms the physical background against which the events of the novel take place
- it provides the circumstances or situation in which the plot develops
- it can portray a particular view of a 'society' and can be linked to particular values or themes.

The grid below provides notes on the settings and contexts of all of the set novels for this unit. Look for the text you are studying.

Novel	Setting and context
Of Mice and Men	set in California during the Great Depression, focusing on the lives of two migrant ranch workers.
Anita and Me	set in a Midlands mining village in the 1970s, focusing on the experiences of a Punjabi girl growing up in the area.
To Kill a Mockingbird	set in a small town in Alabama in the American Deep South during the 1930s; it relates the experiences of a young girl growing up in a society affected by racism and prejudice.
I Know Why the Caged Bird Sings	set in the small town of Stamps, Arkansas, a Southern State in the USA; this autobiographical novel describes the author's life, growing up as an African American in a prejudiced and racist society.
Chandra's Secrets	set in a fictional city in Southern Africa, it tells the story of a sixteen-year-old set against the background of a society affected by HIV/AIDS which is sweeping the continent.

Look at the passage below, which comes from the opening of *To Kill a Mockingbird*.

1. **What overall impression does the writer give of the town?**
2. **Pick out any words or phrases that you think are particularly effective in creating a sense of the setting.**

Maycomb was an old town, but it was a tired old town when I first knew it. In rainy weather the streets turned to red slop; grass grew on the sidewalks, the court-house sagged in the square. Somehow, it was hotter then; a black dog suffered on a summer's day; bony mules hitched to Hoover carts flicked flies in the sweltering shade of the live oaks on the square. Men's stiff collars wilted by nine in the morning. Ladies bathed before noon, after their three o'clock naps, and by nightfall were like soft teacakes with frostings of sweat and sweet talcum.

People moved slowly then. They ambled across the square, shuffled in and out of the stores around it, took their time about everything. A day was twenty-four hours long but seemed longer. There was no hurry, for there was nowhere to go, nothing to buy and no money to buy it with, nothing to see outside the boundaries of Maycomb County.

Now think about the text that you are studying.

1. **Pick out three passages from the novel and read them carefully.**
2. **Explore the ways in which the writer uses language to give a strong impression, picture or feeling about the setting and atmosphere.**
3. **Remember to use specific details from the text to support your ideas.**

Exploring themes

Themes are the ideas that a writer might explore through the novel or poem. Often a writer might want to draw attention to particular ideas or issues so that the reader will think about them. Sometimes writers want to put across particular messages about the issues they explore.

When you are studying your novel it is a good idea to make a list of the main themes or ideas that you identify. It may help you to use a diagram, like the one shown below, to summarize your ideas.

The diagram relates to the key themes in *Of Mice and Men*. Some of the boxes are blank to show that more themes could be added.

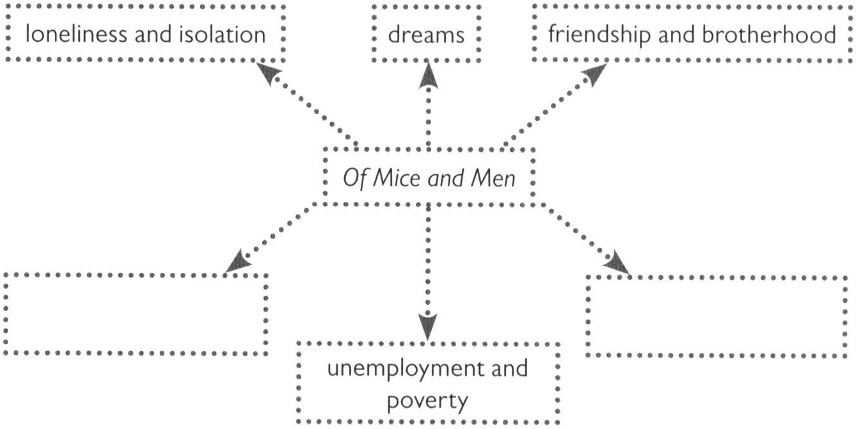

Make a list of four key themes that are explored in the novel you are studying. Make brief notes on the ideas that are suggested and any messages that you think the writer wants to make the reader think about.

Having established what you see as the key themes in your novel, you now need to look at each one in more detail.

The list below suggests some things to think about.

- How does each theme relate to the main storyline?
- What message does the writer want to convey to the reader?
- How does the writer present the themes? You should look at:
  - the language used
  - characters
  - the use of imagery and symbols.

Remember that you should use specific examples from the text to illustrate the points you make.

When making notes on themes it can be useful to keep a log of page references so that you can find the relevant sections easily when you are revising.

Look back at the novel you are studying and use a grid, like the one below, to develop your ideas on the key themes you have identified using examples from the text

Theme	How it is presented	Examples from the text

Unseen poetry

The contemporary poems that you will be asked to compare in Section B of Unit 1 will be **unseen**, which means that you will not know what these poems will be until you open your exam paper. As you will not know what the poems will be in advance you cannot revise specific texts. What you can do, however, is make sure that by the time you get to the exam, you are well-practised and confident in using **close reading skills**.

To close read effectively you will need to have a clear sense of what it is you should be looking for and you will also need a good grasp of what each text is about. The steps below set out how you might approach a close reading in your exam.

1. Read the question

The question will ask you to do three things:

- write about the poems and the **effect** they have on you
- write about how the poems are **similar** and **different**.

2. What are the poems about?

When you are dealing with a text that you have never seen before, the first thing that you need to do is to get a sense of what the overall text is 'about'. In the exam you will be given one or two lines of basic information in the question that will help you with this. This information might tell you who the speaker is in each poem, or where each poem is set. Be sure to read this.

Next, read through the poems. Don't worry if you don't understand every word. Your aim is to get an overall impression of the poem: the subject matter, the key themes, and the speaker's perspective. This means that, when you home in on specific details, you will be aware of how the detail fits in with the rest of the poem.

Practise this skill by selecting two poems from your poetry collection. Write two sentences on each poem, summarizing what the poem is about, where it is set or who is speaking.

3. Identify what to look for

Once you have read the poems once you should go back to the question. This will include a bullet-point list of specific things that you should look for. The question will ask you to write about the similarities and differences between the poems in relation to the following areas:

- what the poems are about (you should already have some sense of this following your first read-through)
- the ideas the poet may have wanted us to think about (you will probably have a sense of this too).
- the mood or atmosphere of the poems
- your responses to the poems
- how the poems are written – words and phrases that you find interesting, the way they are organized and so on.

How the poems are written

Here are some of the features you might comment on when considering how the poems are written:

- the vocabulary the poets use – make a note of any words or phrases that you find particularly effective and the impact of them
- any imagery the poets use such as metaphors, similes and personification
- the use of rhyme and rhythm.

Remember – simply spotting features is not enough – you need to be able to say something about the **effects** created.

4. Annotating the poems

You should now read both poems again and annotate them. Keep the question and bullet points in mind as you read. You should mark specific words or features that you can comment on in your answer.

Look at the tips below on making useful annotations.

- Mark and comment – highlight specific words, features and phrases that strike you as interesting or important.

- Keep your notes short – your annotations should act as starting points for further thinking, so you should keep them concise and aim to expand and develop them in your written answer.

- Be selective – only pick out the features that stand out or mean something to you. Don't highlight every simile and every metaphor that you find. Only mark features that you can relate to the question. Bear in mind that you will have less than an hour to write about both poems, so you won't be able to talk about everything in your response.

- Code your annotations – if you keep it simple, using a code to mark your annotations can make them easier to refer back to when you write your answer. You could use a different mark for each of the points in the question. Look at the example key below.

  Underline text with straight line = for content and the poet's ideas
  Underline text with wobbly line = for mood/atmosphere
  Circle text = for interesting words, poetic devices and structural features
  Box text = where you will make a personal response.

  This approach will help you to cover all of the bullet points given in the question. Whatever point you are focusing on, however, always remember to think about the **similarities** and **differences** between the poems.

Using these guidelines, annotate the two poems that you have selected to practise with.

5. Writing a comparative response

At this point you should identify how the second poem is similar to and different from the first.

You can write your comparison either by:

1. writing about each poem separately and then comparing them. (If you use this method make sure that your comparisons are well-developed in the final section of your response).
2. Making comparisons where appropriate throughout your answer as a whole. (However, avoid playing 'ping pong' between the poems. Make sure your points are well-organized and flow on logically.)

When writing comparatively, there are certain words and phrases that you can use to help you structure your response.

The following phrases can be used when writing about differences:

on the other hand...

however...

compared with...

in contrast to...

whereas...

unlike...

The words and phrases below can be used to suggest similarities:

but...

and...

in the same way...

equally...

Now try a practice exercise using two example poems.

The first poem, *The Farrier* by Owen Sheers describes a blacksmith shoeing a horse. The second, *Jones the Grocer* by Herbert Williams describes a grocer and the shop he used to keep.

Write about both poems and their effect on you. Show how they are similar and how they are different.

You may write about each poem separately and then compare them, or make comparisons where appropriate in your answer as a whole.

You may wish to include some or all of these points:

- *the content of the poem – what they are about;*
- *the ideas the poets may have wanted us to think about;*
- *the mood or atmosphere of the poems;*
- *how they are written – words and phrases you find interesting, the way they are organized, and so on;*
- *your responses to the poems.* [20]

The Farrier

Blessing himself with his apron,
the leather black and tan of a rain-beaten bay,
he pinches a roll-up to his lips and waits

for the mare to be led from the field to the yard,
the smoke slow-turning from his mouth
and the wind twisting his sideburns in its fingers.

She smells him as he passes, woodbine, metal and hoof,
careful not to look her in the eye as he runs his hand
the length of her neck, checking for dust on a lintel.

Folding her back leg with one arm, he leans into her flank
like a man putting his shoulders to a knackered car,
catches the hoof between his knees

as is it's always just fallen from a table,
cups her fetlock and bends,
a romantic lead dropping to the lips of his lover.

Then the close work begins; cutting moon-sliver clippings
excavating the arrow head of her frog,
filing at her sole and branding on a shoe

in an apparition of smoke,
three nails gritted between his teeth,
a seamstress pinning the dress on the bride.

Placing his tools in their beds,
he gives her a slap and watches her leave,
awkward in her new shoes, walking on strange ground.

The sound of his steel, biting at her heels.

Owen Sheers

Jones the Grocer

Jones the Grocer, we called him –
A pale man, skilled in servility,
His hands white and soft as the lard he stacked
In small meticulous rows, his head
Polished and somehow apologetic, as if
He was crowned forever with dishonour.

I hated him, he was too obsequious by far,
Embellishing transactions with fulsome flattery
Of your habits, your appearance, your miserable opinions.
He seemed to exist in a fog
Of self-effacement, through which one caught
The rarest glimpse of human dignity.

Yet one could suffer the arid washing of his hands
For the joy of that shop, its curiosities,
Like the corner where it was always dusk
And equatorial, aromatic with coffee beans,
And calendars derisive of popularity,
And the adverts twenty years out of date.

One could suffer it, and gladly suffer it again
To be delivered of this, its successor –
A supermarket, slick and soulless,
Arrogantly accepting the shoppers' homage.

Herbert Williams

The steps below suggest one method of approaching this task:

1. read both poems through carefully with a pen in your hand to make notes. Get an overall sense of what each poem is about and how the poems are written
2. re-read 'The Farrier' and annotate the poem
3. re-read and annotate 'Jones the Grocer'
4. make two lists – one of similarities and the other of differences, noting your key points
5. number the points to show how you intend to structure your response.

Writing your response

The diagram below shows one way to structure your responses.

Introduction – comment on what each poem is about.

↓

Main body of the answer consisting of:

- your comments on the first poem
- your comments on the second poem
- reference back to the first poem whenever you think it's relevant.

↓

Conclusion – sum-up your ideas and include your own personal response with any further comparisons.

Boost your grade

In order to achieve the best possible grade in Unit 1 you should:

- make sure that you **know your texts** very well
- be aware of the **ideas and themes** raised in your texts and **how language is used** to present these
- understand how **setting** is important and how the writers present it
- be comfortable **comparing texts**
- understand how **context** is significant in the text you have studied.

Section A: Individual texts in context

To perform well in Section A of this unit you should:

- have a **good overview** of the texts
- have a **detailed understanding of the characters** in your texts and be able to discuss them thoroughly, **evaluating their actions**, **relationships**, **attitudes** and **motives**
- understand the **themes and ideas** explored in the texts
- understand the importance of **settings** and how settings are presented in your texts
- show a clear understanding of **social, cultural and historical contexts** relevant to your texts
- put your ideas across in a **convincing** and **persuasive** way
- use **well-chosen textual references** to support your ideas
- **write clearly and fluently** with few mistakes in **spelling**, **punctuation** and **grammar**.

Section B: Comparative study

To boost your performance in Section B of this unit you should:

- be able to **discuss the poems in detail**
- identify **themes and ideas** explored in the poems
- comment on and **compare** the **language** and **style** of the poems
- make **detailed links** and **comparisons** between the unseen poems you are given in the exam
- compare the **subject**, **themes** and **overall effects** of the poems
- use **carefully chosen details** from the poems to illustrate the points you make
- put your ideas across in a **convincing** and **persuasive** way
- **write clearly and fluently** with few mistakes in **spelling**, **punctuation** and **grammar**.

Unit 2: Drama and Prose

Exam insight

Unit summary

This unit is divided into two options and you will take one of them.

Unit 2a: Literary Heritage Drama and Contemporary Prose

Or

Unit 2b: Contemporary Drama and Literary Heritage Prose

Unit 2a: Literary Heritage Drama and Contemporary Prose

Unit 2a is assessed by an exam lasting **2 hours** and it is worth 40% of your marks for this GCSE.

For this paper you will study a drama text from the English/Irish/Welsh literary heritage and a contemporary prose text. Both texts must be chosen from the list provided by the exam board.

In the exam you will need to answer **two** questions on each text.

The first question on each text, part (i), will require you to carry out a **close reading** of an extract from the text. You should spend 20 minutes on this task.

The second question on each text will give you a choice of tasks, parts (ii) and (iii), which will relate to each **text as a whole**. You should answer **one** of these questions and you should spend 40 minutes on your response to it.

Unit 2b: Contemporary Drama and Literary Heritage Prose

Unit 2b follows the same structure as Unit 2a but you will study a contemporary drama text and a literary heritage prose text. Both texts must be chosen from the list provided by the exam board.

For both Unit 2a and Unit 2b you will not be allowed to take copies of the texts you have studied into the exam with you.

Assessment Objectives

Questions on contemporary texts

The questions on contemporary texts will test the Assessment Objectives set out below.

Question 1, part (i), will test your ability to:

AO1

Respond to texts critically and imaginatively; select and evaluate relevant textual detail to illustrate and support interpretations.

This means that you will need to show in your answer that you have read your text carefully and are able to comment on aspects of it such as **characters**, **relationships**, **attitudes** and **motives**. You will need to use **carefully selected details** from the text to support your ideas.

AO2

Explain how language, structure and form contribute to writers' presentations of ideas, themes and settings.

This means that you will look at the **different ways** writers **use language** to **achieve effects** and comment on stylistic features to show how they affect meaning.

Question 2, parts (ii) and (iii), will also test AO1 and AO2.

Questions on literary heritage texts

The questions on your literary heritage text will test the Assessment Objectives explained below.

Question 1, part (i), will test your ability to:

AO1

Respond to texts critically and imaginatively; select and evaluate relevant textual detail to illustrate and support interpretations.

This means that you will need to show in your answer that you have read your text carefully and are able to comment on aspects of it such as **characters**, **relationships**, **attitudes** and **motives**. You will need to use **carefully selected details** from the text to support your ideas.

AO2

Explain how language, structure and form contribute to writers' presentations of ideas, themes and settings.

This means that you will look at the **different ways** writers **use language** to **achieve effects** and comment on stylistic features to show how they affect meaning.

Question 2, parts (ii) and (iii), will test AO1 and AO4.

AO4

Relate texts to their social, cultural and historical context; explain how texts have been influential and significant to yourself and other readers in different contexts and at different times.

This means that you will examine how different factors, such as the **historical period**, **social** and **cultural factors**, can **influence the way a text is written** and relate this to the affect the text has on the reader.

Literary heritage drama and contemporary prose texts (Unit 2a)

Literary heritage drama texts include a range of titles by different writers. They fall into the 'literary heritage' category for a number of reasons. Most of them have been read and performed for many years and they are often considered to have had an impact on shaping the way that English drama has developed over time. If you are taking the Unit 2a option, you will focus on one of the following texts:

Othello	William Shakespeare
Much Ado About Nothing	William Shakespeare
An Inspector Calls	J.B. Priestley
Hobson's Choice	Harold Brighouse
A Taste of Honey	Shelagh Delaney

Contemporary prose texts are texts that have been written in fairly recent times. For Unit 2a, you will focus on one of the texts below:

Paddy Clarke Ha Ha Ha	Roddy Doyle
Heroes	Robert Cormier
Never Let Me Go	Kazuo Ishiguro
About a Boy	Nick Hornby
Resistance	Owen Sheers

Contemporary drama and literary heritage prose texts (Unit 2b)

Contemporary drama texts include plays that have been written in relatively recent times and deal with modern themes. If you are taking the Unit 2b option, you will focus on one of the texts below:

The History Boys	Alan Bennett
Blood Brothers	Willy Russell
A View from the Bridge	Arthur Miller
Be My Baby	Amanda Whittington
My Mother Said I Never Should	Charlotte Keatley

Literary heritage prose texts include novels that are considered to be influential in terms of the way that literary prose has developed over time. These texts have been read and enjoyed for decades. If you are taking the Unit 2b option, you will study one of the following texts:

Silas Marner	George Eliot
Pride and Prejudice	Jane Austen
A Christmas Carol	Charles Dickens
Lord of the Flies	William Golding
Ash on a Young Man's Sleeve	Dannie Abse

Approaching your prose text

Question Structure

You will answer **two** questions on each text: the first consists of one part, the second consists of two options.

Question 1, part (i)

This will be based on an extract from the text you have studied. There will be one extract-based question per text. It could focus on one of a range of topics such as:

- the presentation of a character:
  - how he or she speaks
  - how he or she behaves
  - how the writer presents the character's thoughts and feelings
  - how the writer influences the reader's attitude towards the character
- how mood and atmosphere is created
- your own response:
  - what you think and feel as you read the extract.

You will need to base your answer closely on the specific extract printed on your exam paper. Remember to support your ideas with well-chosen references to the extract.

Question 2, parts (ii) and (iii)

Following the extract-based question, you will be given a choice of two questions and you should answer only **one** of them. This question could ask you about:

- characters and the ways they are presented
- a character's relationship with another character
- which character you sympathize with most and why
- how effective the title of your text is
- how the writer presents certain aspects of a character
- which aspect of your text you have found most interesting and why
- how a certain setting is important to the novel as a whole
- how the writer presents a particular theme
- how a character changes throughout the novel
- the extent to which you agree with a statement about the text.

Close reading: prose

Narrative voice

When studying your prose text, one of the first things you should do is familiarize yourself with the plot of the novel. This will allow you to develop an important overview of the text as a whole. You should also make yourself aware of how the writer tells the story. Is the story told from a first-person perspective using 'I', 'me' or 'we'? Or has the writer chosen to write the story from a third-person perspective as if he or she is an observer outside the story?

Note the points below about first-person and third-person narration.

First-person narration:

- tells you what is happening as seen through the eyes of one of the characters
- seems to address you directly
- has a limited point of view because the narrator cannot know what other characters are thinking.

Third-person narration:

- allows the reader to see and know everything that the writer wants them to – in this case the narrator is known as an 'omniscient narrator'.

The way that the writer tells the story is referred to as the 'narrative voice'.

Look at the extract belowand on the next page. What do you notice about the narrative voice in each extract?

Text A

I preferred magnifying glasses to matches. We spent afternoons burning little piles of cut grass. I loved watching the grass change colour. I loved it when the flame began to race through the grass. You had more control with a magnifying glass. It was easier but it took more skill. If the sun stayed out long enough you could saw through a sheet of paper and not have to touch it, just put down a stone in each corner to stop it from blowing away. We'd have a race; burn, blow it out, burn, blow it out. Last to burn the paper completely in half had to let the other fella burn his hand. We'd draw a man on the paper and burn holes in him; in his hands and his feet, like Jesus. We drew long hair on him. We left his mickey till last.

From *Paddy Clarke Ha Ha Ha* by Roddy Doyle

Text B

It was fifteen years since Silas Marner had first come to Raveloe; he was then simply a pallid young man, with prominent, short-sighted brown eyes, whose appearance would have had nothing strange for people of average culture and experience, but for the villagers near whom he had come to settle it had mysterious peculiarities which corresponded with the exceptional nature of his occupation, and his advent from an unknown region called 'North'ard.' So had his way of life:—he invited no comer to step across his door-sill, and he never strolled into the village to drink a pint at the Rainbow, or to gossip at the wheelwright's: he sought no man or woman, save for the purposes of his calling, or in order to supply himself with necessaries; and it was soon clear to the Raveloe lasses that he would never urge one of them to accept him against her will—quite as if he had heard them declare that they would never marry a dead man come to life again.

From *Silas Marner* by George Eliot

Analysing characters

Look back at the extract from *Paddy Clarke Ha Ha Ha* and the extract from *Silas Marner* and think about the following points:

- **what** each reveals about the characters
- **how** each writer presents this
- the effects created by each writer's language choices in terms of presenting the characters.

Consider the novel you are studying and choose an extract from it in which a particular character is a key focus. This passage should be about thirty lines long.

Remember that characters can be presented in various ways, such as:

- description – the language the writer uses
- dialogue – what the characters say, how they speak, what other characters say about them
- thoughts and feelings – revealed directly either through speech or through the narrator
- action and reactions – how the characters behave and react to situations or other characters.

Now write your response to this question:

Look closely at how the writer presents the character or characters here. How does this passage influence the reader's attitude to the character or characters.

Setting

The setting is the 'world' in which the story of the novel is set. The setting can be important in several ways:

- it can form the background or physical surroundings against which the action of the story takes place
- it can reflect the characters and their experiences
- it can be closely linked to the theme(s) the writer presents and explores
- it can portray a particular society, culture and values.

Themes

Themes are the ideas or messages that writers present and explore in their novels. The themes often lie behind the story as a whole and are developed throughout it. A novel might explore one key theme or it might explore several. Themes can be ideas the writers want their readers to think about or messages they want to put across to them.

1. Look at the key themes presented in the novel you are studying and make a list of them.
2. Pick the theme that you think is most significant or interesting.
3. Now try answering the following question:

How does the writer present the theme in the novel?

Mood and atmosphere

The mood and atmosphere of a novel is often closely linked to the setting and the feelings and actions of the characters. Writers very often use stylistic techniques and careful language choices to create a sense of mood and atmosphere.

Here are some of the techniques that writers can use:

- **action** – what's happening in the text
- **characters** – what the characters are doing and thinking?
- **setting** – where the action takes place
- **vocabulary choices** – using words and phrases to help suggest a particular mood
- **dialogue** – not only conveys information but can also establish a specific tone
- **repetition** – of word and phrases
- **imagery** – including similes, metaphors and personification
- **phonological features** – including alliteration, onomatopoeia and assonance
- **symbols and motifs** – words, ideas and images that are repeatedly used in your text
- **use of the senses** – such as smell, touch and sound.

Look at the extract below from *Great Expectations*

How does the writer use language to create a sense of setting and atmosphere here?

Use specific examples to illustrate and support your ideas.

Ours was the marsh country, down by the river, within, as the river wound, twenty miles of the sea. My first most vivid and broad impression of the identity of things, seems to me to have been gained on a memorable raw afternoon towards evening. At such a time I found out for certain, that this bleak place overgrown with nettles was the churchyard; and that Philip Pirrip, late of this parish, and also Georgina wife of the above, were dead and buried; and that Alexander, Batholomew, Abraham, Tobias and Roger, infant children of the aforesaid, were also dead and buried; and that the dark flat wilderness beyond the churchyard, intersected with dykes and mounds and gates, with scattered cattle feeding on it, was the marshes; and that the low leaden line beyond, was the river; and that the distant savage lair from which the wind was rushing, was the sea; and that the small bundle of shivers growing afraid of it all and beginning to cry, was Pip.

From *Great Expectations* by Charles Dickens

Select an extract from the novel which presents setting effectively. With close reference to the extract, show how the writer creates mood and atmosphere.

Approaching your drama text

The drama questions in this Unit will be divided into three parts. You will need to answer part (i) and either part (ii) or part (iii). Part (i) will be based on an extract from the text you have studied. Part (ii) and (iii) will be based on the text as a whole.

Part (i)

You will be given one question for part (i) of the exam. The question will be based on an extract from the text and could ask you about various topics, including:

- the presentation of a character or characters
- how relationships between characters are revealed
- how characters speak and behave
- how characters reveal their feelings
- how an audience might respond to characters or feel about them
- how mood and atmosphere are created.

Remember that, when answering this question, you need to focus your answer closely on the extract you are given rather than writing generally on the play as a whole.

Parts (ii) and (iii)

This section of the exam will give you a choice of two tasks, both of which will relate to the text as a whole. You should answer only **one** of these questions.

Here are some things you might be asked about:

- why a character acts in a particular way in the play
- how a character is presented to the audience throughout the play (or changes during the course of the play)
- how relationships between characters are developed
- how relevant the play is to a modern audience
- why particular characters are important to the play as a whole
- how relevant the play's title is to the play.

Studying drama

When studying a drama text it is important to keep in mind that drama texts are usually written to be seen in performance rather than read.

It will really help your study of the text if you can see a performance of it. If you cannot see a live performance on stage, try to watch it on DVD or listen to an audio recording.

The plan below suggests one way that you might approach the study of your play.

1. Read the whole play. Reading it aloud with others taking parts will help to bring the play to life. Making brief notes or summaries of scenes is a useful way to get an overall picture of the plot and characters.
2. Once you have read the play, you can look at it in more detail:
   - make notes on the characters – who they are, what they do
   - look at the key speeches of the main characters
   - think about the ideas or themes explored in the play
   - think about how the play is structured – the way that the events of the plot link together
   - look carefully at the language of the play, including the dialogue, soliloquies and what these reveal about the characters and themes
   - look at the stage directions and what they tell you.
3. Putting together notes on the following topics can also help you to develop a deeper understanding of your play:
   - act/scene summaries
   - notes on key speeches
   - a character log with notes on key turning points in character development and significant quotations
   - list of key themes.

Close reading: drama

The opening of a play is very important because it is vital that the writer captures the audience's interest and attention.

The opening scene can:

- give background information about the plot, e.g. an explanation of what has gone on before the play opens
- create a setting or background against which the action of the play is set
- establish a particular mood or atmosphere, e.g. a sense of tension
- introduce a key character or characters, or indicate a particular situation or relationship
- create a sense of mystery to intrigue the audience and make them want to know more.

Whatever play you are studying for this unit, the key questions you need to ask yourself in regards to the opening scene are:

1. What effect does the writer want this scene to have on the audience?

2. What purpose does the scene have in the context of the play as a whole?

Look carefully at the opening scene of the play you are studying.

Make notes on:

1. **how the play opens**
2. **what you think the writer wants to achieve here**
3. **what effect it has on the audience.**

Analysing characters

The points below suggest things to look for when analysing the characters in the play you are studying.

- **Stage directions** – sometimes dramatists give important information about their characters in stage directions. When studying a play, you will read these directions but when you watch a play you will see them perfomed.
- **Dialogue** – what the characters say will be of key importance. Consider how closely characters' words match-up with their actions and what characters say about each other.
- **Soliloquies and asides** – can reveal the inner thoughts and feelings of the speaker.
    - **Asides** are short comments spoken by a character so that other characters cannot hear them but the audience can. Dramatists can use this technique to give away small but important plot details to the audience. Asides can also reveal things about the character speaking.
    - **Soliloquies** are usually longer and more developed speeches where the character is alone on stage or at least out of earshot of the other characters. Dramatists often use soliloquies to grant the audience an insight into the deepest thoughts of their characters.

Look at the play you are studying and think about the key characters.

For each character make a character 'log' in which you record key points about the character's actions, traits and development in the play together with evidence to support and illustrate your points.

You could record the information in a grid like the one below to help you when you come to revise:

Character		
Act/scene	**Point**	**Evidence/quotation**

Themes

Almost all plays explore wider ideas or issues in some way. You should try to identify what the key ideas or themes are early on in your study of the play.

Here are some ways in which dramatists can present themes:

- through the dialogue that occurs between characters
- through what the characters do
- through showing how characters relate to one another
- through key speeches in the play
- through the use of imagery
- through the use of symbolism
- through the use of setting.

1. Decide on what you think the main theme is in the play you are studying.

2. Write about the way this theme is presented in the play.

Make sure that you look at the full range of methods and techniques the dramatist uses to present the theme. Remember to support your ideas with references to the text.

Setting, mood and atmosphere

What happens in the play, as well as what the characters do and say and the language they use, are all likley to contribute to the setting, mood and atmosphere of the text. The list below suggests some other points to think about when considering the setting.

- **The stage set** – gives a sense of setting and can suggest a particular atmosphere. (When reading the text, information regarding this is often given in the form of stage directions). In some plays stage directions are very detailed, in others they are more minimal.
- **Lighting** – this can be used to create all kinds of effects and can influence the mood and atmosphere enormously.
- **Sound effects** – these can also add greatly to the impact of the drama, for example, when creating a storm scene, lighting and sound can combine to create a vivid sense of the scene. Music too can be an important feature.
- **Props** – these can be used in different ways to add effect.

Remember – when analysing the dramatic techniques used to create a sense of setting, mood or atmosphere, look at how features work together to produce an overall effect.

Think about the text you are studying and choose an extract of about 30–40 lines, that you feel creates a strong sense of mood and atmosphere.

With close reference to the extract, show how the dramatist creates mood and atmosphere for an audience here.

Social, cultural and historical contexts

When studying your **literary heritage text**, one of the Assessment Objectives tested through your response is AO4; your ability to link the text to the relevant social, cultural and historical contexts.

Contexts are factors that influence the way that writers write texts and also how texts are interpreted by the reader. Many contexts can impact upon how a text is written, such as:

- the life and background of the writer; (remember, however, that your focus should be the text, not the life story of the writer)
- the historical period in which the text was written
- the culture or society within which the text was written
- the wider themes, ideas or issues raised in the text.

Boost your grade

In order to achieve the best possible grade in Unit 2 you should:

- **know your texts** very well
- give your **opinions** on **characters**, **context**, **settings** and **themes**
- understand **how** the writers **use language** and dramatic and stylistic features **to create effects**
- use **details** from the text to **support** and illustrate your ideas
- be able to present your ideas **clearly** and **logically**.

Contemporary prose or drama questions

To do well in the exam, when producing a critical response to your contemporary text, you need to:

- make **detailed references** to the text
- be prepared to **offer judgements**
- be able to evaluate the **attitudes and relationships of characters**
- select and evaluate **relevant textual details** to illustrate your ideas
- show how writers use **ideas, themes and settings** to **create effects**
- convey your ideas **clearly** and **persuasively**
- **write clearly**, **fluently** and **accurately**.

Literary heritage texts

When studying literary heritage texts you will also need to demonstrate an understanding of the relevant **social, cultural and historical contexts**. To do well in this area of the assessment, you need to:

- show a clear understanding of what the **social, cultural and historical contexts** of your text are
- be able to understand **how** the reader's understanding of the text might be influenced by context
- be able to **relate the text** to your **own and others' experiences**.

Unit 3: Poetry and Drama (Literary Heritage)

Controlled Assessment insight

Unit summary

This unit is worth 25% of your GCSE.

Studying Shakespeare and linked poetry

Your assessment for this unit will be based on one assignment in which you will link a play by Shakespeare with literary heritage poetry.

You will study one Shakespeare play (excluding *Othello* or *Much Ado about Nothing*) and a group of poems, linked by theme, from the WJEC poetry collection.

The exam board will supply generic tasks and your teacher will adapt them to suit the texts you have studied. The texts you write about will be **linked by theme**.

The tasks may be based on thematic areas such as: love, family and parent/child relationships, youth/age, power/ambition, male/female relationships/role of women, hypocrisy/prejudice, conflict and grief.

Approaching the Controlled Assessment

This unit is assessed by Controlled Assessment. This means that you will be able to prepare for your assignment in lessons but you will write your final response under formal supervision. The points below explain the stages of the Controlled Assessment

1. Your Controlled Assessment will begin with a research and planning stage during which you will work under limited supervision. During this stage you will be able to work with other students and have access to reference materials.
2. You will then write your final assignment under formal supervision and will be allowed up to a total of **four hours** for this stage. During this stage of the assessment you will **not** be allowed to discuss your response with other students or request guidance from your teacher.
3. The writing stage of your assessment may be divided into a number of shorter sessions. If this is the case then your work will be collected in at the end of each session. You will not be allowed to amend your work once you have handed it in at the end of the final session.
4. You are allowed to take clean copies of your texts and **one A4 sheet of your own notes** into the assessment with you.

Assessment Objectives

Unit 3 will be assessed according to the following Assessment Objectives:

AO1

Respond to texts critically and imaginatively; select and evaluate relevant textual detail to illustrate and support interpretations.

This means that you will need to show in your answer that you have **read your texts closely** and are able to comment on aspects of them such as the **attitudes**, **motives** and **relationships of characters**. You will need to use **carefully-selected details** from the text to illustrate and **support your ideas**.

AO2

Explain how language, structure and form contribute to writers' presentations of ideas, themes and settings.

This means that you will look at the different ways **writers use language** to **achieve effects**.

AO3

Make comparisons and explain links between texts, evaluating writers' different ways of expressing meaning and achieving effects.

This means that you will **compare** the ways in which writers have used **language and different techniques** to express **meaning** in the texts you have studied.

Studying your Shakespeare play

When approaching your play remember that Shakespeare's plays, like any other plays, were written to be seen in performance rather than being read in a classroom. While reading the play always try to think about how it might work on stage.

In order to write effectively about your play in your assessment you first need to arrive at a detailed understanding of it.

Here are some things you can do to achieve this:

- read the whole play closely
- if you can, read the play as a group
- make brief notes on each scene as you go through to help you develop an overall impression of the plot
- make notes on the characters and how they relate to each other
- imagine the action in your mind as you read each scene
- make a list of the key themes and ideas explored in the play
- if you can, see the play performed – either a live version or a recording.

Make notes on how the play you are studying explores the theme you are focusing on. Write down your ideas with examples and quotations.

Shakespeare's language

Shakespeare uses different forms of language at different points in the play. For example:

1. **Verse** – there are two types of verse. Blank verse is unrhymed verse that uses iambic pentameter (ten syllables a line consisting of an unstressed syllable followed by a stressed syllable). Most of Shakespeare's plays are written in this form of verse. The other form is rhymed verse. This is often used at the end of scenes where rhyming couplets are used to draw the scene to a close. Sometimes rhymed verse is also used for dramatic effect.

2. **Prose** – is used in various contexts by characters of all kinds. Depending on the speaker, it can be used to reveal heightened emotions, such as desperation, regret or grief; or it can be used to distinguish characters considered to be of a lower social status.

When commenting on Shakespeare's use of language, the key is to look at the specific context in which Shakespeare uses it. What is happening at that point in the play, and how does Shakespeare's choice of language help to convey meaning?

Analysing character

An essential part of the study of your play will be to understand how Shakespeare presents his characters and to look at how Shakespeare uses language in relation to this.

The list below suggests things you might consider.

- Physical descriptions of characters – sometimes given in stage directions.
- What characters say and how they say it.
- What characters think (look for soliloquies and asides).
- How characters behave and respond to other characters.
- What is revealed about the motives of characters.
- How characters change (either in different situations or as the play goes on).

Studying linked poems

Themes in poetry

Your work on the poetry in this unit will be focused on a particular theme. The relevant themes for this unit are as follows:

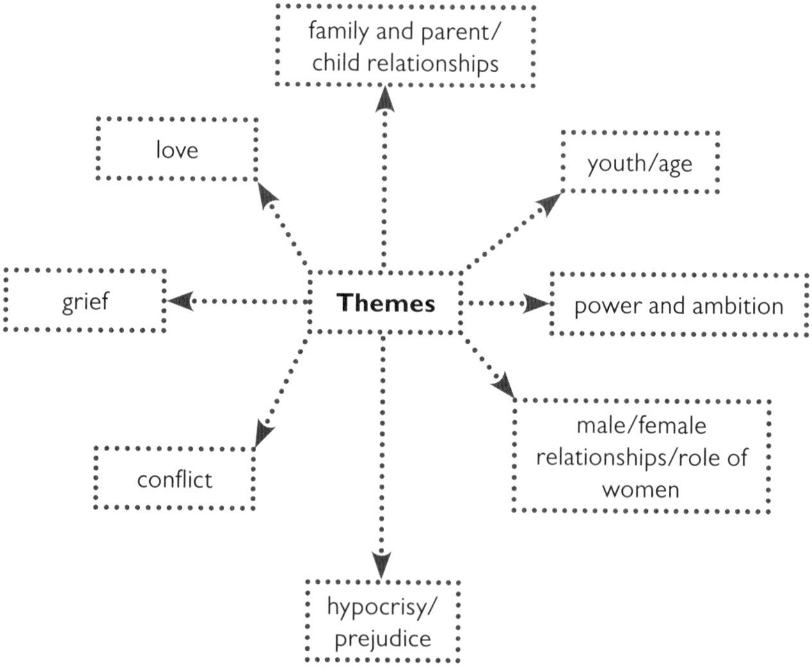

Your task will be to examine how one of these themes is important in your chosen poems and also link this to the way the theme is handled in the Shakespeare play you have studied.

Approaching your poems

Start off with the whole collection of poems for this unit and try to read as many of them as you can during your course. Enjoy reading the poems, keeping in mind any links that occur to you. Practise writing about the poems in class. You will have a clean copy of the poetry collection and the Shakespeare text for the Controlled Assessment.

The steps below set out one possible approach to studying a selection of poems in more detail.

1. Look carefully at the task and think about the theme and what ideas this involves.
2. Select poems that you might focus on particularly for your Controlled Assessment. (To some extent the length of the poems could affect the number you choose for more detailed study.)
3. Re-read your chosen poems several times and make notes on each poem about how it is relevant to the theme you are focusing on. Make use of your knowledge and understanding of the play you have studied and other poems from the collection.
4. Now look at each poem in more detail. You need to consider the following elements in regards to your theme:

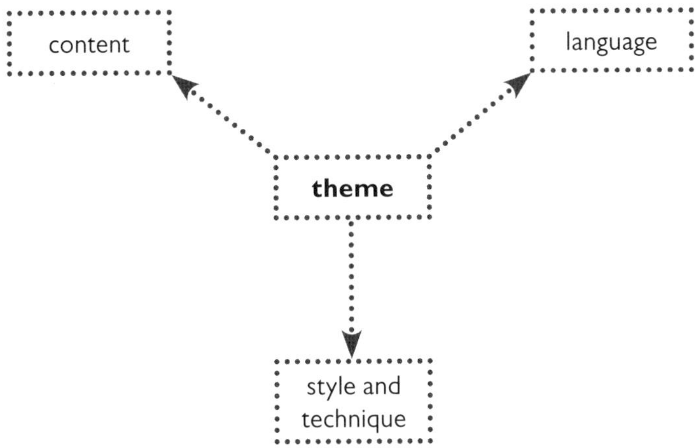

Making links between poetry and drama

Before you start to write your assessment you need to draw together your ideas on your Shakespeare play and the poems you have studied.

Think about the questions below.

The Shakespeare play

1. How is the theme you have studied explored in the **content** of the play?
   - Make a list of the key points.
   - Give evidence and quotations to support your points.
2. How does Shakespeare use **characters** to present ideas about the theme?
   - Make a note of characters or events involving characters that you think are key to the theme you are studying.
   - Make a note of how characters are presented – remember to look at **how** Shakespeare presents them.
3. Are other features such as setting, mood and atmosphere important in relation to your chosen theme?
   - Make a note of any other features that you think are important.
4. What are your views on the play and the way that your chosen theme is presented and explored?

Remember – your own views are very important – be confident with your ideas, and make sure that you can explain and support them.

Using the ideas above, think about the play that you have studied and make notes on it. Include ideas on your own responses to the play and provide examples to support your views.

The poems

1. How is your chosen theme explored in the **content** of the poems?
   - Make a list of the main points from each poem.
   - Think about how the theme is perhaps dealt with differently in different poems.
2. How do the poets use **characters** or **personas** to explore the theme?
   - Make a note of how the writers make use of voice to explore the theme.
   - Identify how language is used in each case.
3. Are other features such as setting, mood or atmosphere important?
   - Make a note of any other features that are relevant to your chosen theme.
4. What is your personal view on the poems?

The task

Your teacher will receive a generic task set by the exam board and will adapt this into a specific task to suit the texts that you have studied. The question may, for example, make reference to particular poems, parts of the play or specific characters.

An example of a specific task is given below.

- How does Shakespeare present power and ambition in Macbeth throughout the play?
- The theme of power and ambition is also present in a number of the poems you have studied. Discuss the way power and ambition is presented in the poetry you have studied.
- What is your personal response to the literature you have studied? In your answer you must explore the links between the poetry and the Shakespeare play.

Using the play and the poems you have studied try writing a response to one of the tasks. You may need to select a different theme to suit your texts.

Preparing your A4 notes

When writing your assignment for your Controlled Assessment you are allowed to refer to a clean copy of the texts plus one A4 side of **your own** notes. A 'clean copy' of a text simply means a text without any notes or annotations on it.

Your notes must:

- have been prepared entirely by you, without help from anyone else
- not contain a draft of your assignment.

Your notes may be either handwritten or typed. Your teacher may check your notes to make sure that they are acceptable before your go into your Controlled Assessment.

What your notes can contain

Your notes can include:

- the exact title of your task
- page references of particular parts of the text you want to refer to while writing your assignment
- key quotations
- the names of characters you wish to focus on
- points to jog your memory
- spellings of particular words.

Look at the examples of notes below. The first set represents the kind of notes that are acceptable and the second set represents the kind of notes that are not. Both sets of notes relate to the sample task below and apply to *Romeo & Juliet* by Shakespeare and the poem 'Drummer Hodge' by Thomas Hardy.

> Many of the plays and poems are concerned with conflict and its results. Choose one particular conflict in the drama you have studied and link it with how conflict and its results are presented in the poetry you have studied.

These notes are acceptable

References

DRAMA

Prologue intro re conflict background p18

Tybalt's attitude to Romeo (Act 1, Scene 5, lines 53–91)

Tybalt and Romeo fight (Act 3, Scene 1, lines 35–135)

Consequences of conflict – climax (Act 5, Scene 1)

Pointlessness of conflict – Montague/Capulet/Prince's closing words (Act 5, Scene 1)

POETRY

Hodge's burial – lack of dignity, stanza 1.

Far from home – stanza 2.

Nature and heavens – stanza 3.

Key quotations

DRAMA

"TYBALT: ...Now by the stock and honour of my kin.
To strike him dead I hold it not a sin" (Act 1, Scene 5, lines 53–58)

"CAPULET: As rich shall Romeo by his lady lie,
Poor sacrifices of our enmity." (Act 5, Scene 3, lines 302–303)

POETRY

"They throw in Drummer Hodge...uncoffined (lines 1–2)

"Fresh from his Wessex home–" (line 8)

"And strange-eyed constellations reign/His stars eternally." (lines 17–18)

PLAN

1. Look at the opening of the play and the fight between the servants.
2. Examine Tybalt's view of Romeo as seen at the party.
3. The death of Romeo and Juliet and their destruction resulting from the family quarrel.
4. Waste is also seen in 'Drummer Hodge'.
5. His death far from home not understanding why he was there.
6. He is 'absorbed' by nature – permanent as opposed to transitory human life.

Act, scene or line references are okay, as are quotes and memory joggers.

These notes are not acceptable

Detailed plans and drafts of parts of the essay are not allowed.

COMPARE THE TEXTS:

Opening

The opening lines as delivered by the Chorus set the scene for the play and introduce the key idea of conflict between the warring families, ...

Conclusion

In conclusion, both the play and Drummer Hodge highlight the waste of young life as a result of conflict. The conflict only brings suffering and loss to everyone involved.

Boost your grade

Studying Poetry and Drama (Literary Heritage)

To boost your grade for Unit 3 you must:

- show a clear understanding of your **drama text and the poetry** you have studied
- make convincing critical comments on **how language is used** to convey meaning
- show a **careful** and **detailed** consideration of the ways in which the texts you have studied are **linked thematically**
- comment on the **effects created** by particular **words** and **phrases**
- use **carefully chosen references** from the text to support and illustrate your ideas
- give a **personal response** to the literature you have studied.

You need to:

respond critically

↓

examine the **language** and **organization** of the text

↓

make **links** across your texts

Your work will be marked on how well you meet the demands of three Assessment Objectives: AO1, AO2, AO3.

To achieve the best grade you will need to:

Respond critically to texts

- make **detailed references** to the texts using **carefully-selected** and relevant details
- evaluate the **attitudes**, **motives** and **relationships of characters**
- **range across texts** with confidence
- show that you have an **overview** of the texts and that you are able to move from specific detail to wider ideas
- put your points across in a **clear** and **persuasive way**

Comment on language and organization

- show an appreciation of **how writers use language** to achieve specific effects
- explore and evaluate how **meaning**, **ideas**, and **feelings** are conveyed through **language**, **structure** and **form**.

Make links and comparisons

- write a sustained response focusing on the **links** between the texts
- **select appropriate details** from the texts and **cross-reference** your ideas
- make perceptive, probing **points of comparison**.

Glossary

Adjective: a word that describes a noun – e.g. *the wooden table*; *the red balloon*. They can also indicate degree, e.g. *the tallest girl was the slowest*.

Adverb: a word that describes the action of a verb – e.g. *the boy ate hungrily*.

Allegory: a story or narrative that has a deeper meaning below the surface action, e.g. *Animal Farm* by George Orwell.

Alliteration: the repetition of the same consonant sound, especially at the beginning of words. For example, 'five miles meandering with a mazy motion' (*Kubla Khan* by Samuel Taylor Coleridge).

Allusion: a reference to another event, person, place or work of literature to add meaning to the message, idea, point or theme.

Antithesis: contrasting ideas or words that are balanced against each other, e.g. 'To be, or not to be' (*Hamlet* by William Shakespeare).

Assonance: the repetition of similar vowel sounds. For example, 'there must be Gods thrown down and trumpets blown' ('Hyperion' by John Keats). This shows the paired assonance of *must*, *trum* and *thrown*, *blown*.

Atmosphere: the mood created by a piece of writing.

Audience: the person or people who read, watch or listen to a text. The 'audience' of prose texts are often referred to as 'readers'. The audience of a drama text is always referred to as 'the audience'.

Bathos: an anti-climax or sudden descent from the serious to the ridiculous.

Blank verse: unrhymed poetry consisting of iambic pentameter (a ten-syllable line consisting of an unstressed syllable followed by a stressed one.

Caesura: a deliberate break in a line of poetry.

Colloquial: slang or non-standard features in speech or writing.

Conjunction: a word that connects other words, e.g. *and*, *but*.

Context: the background to a text, both in terms of when and where it was written and when and where the events of the text are set. Factors such as geographical location, time period and the author's personal background can heavily influence how texts are written and understood.

Contraction: a shortened word, e.g. *isn't*, *don't*.

Dialect: a language variety marked by distinctive grammar and vocabulary choices, often used by people with a common regional background.

Dialogue: speech between two or more people.

Elegy: a sad, reflective poem often concerned with death.

Empathy: a feeling the reader experiences when understanding a particular experience of a character or writer.

Free verse: verse written without any fixed structure.

Genre: a particular kind of writing, e.g. prose, poetry, drama.

Hyperbole: a deliberate and extravagant exaggeration.

Imagery: the use of words to create a picture or 'image' in the mind of the reader. Images can relate to any of the senses – not just sight, but also hearing, taste, touch and smell. The term is often used to refer to the use of descriptive language, particularly to the use of **metaphors** and **similes**.

Internal rhyme: words that rhyme within a line rather than at the end of lines.

Metaphor: a comparison of one thing to another in order to make description more vivid. Unlike a **simile**, a metaphor states that one thing *is* the other. For example, a simile could be *The wind cut through me like a knife*, whereas the metaphor might state *The wind cut through me.*

Narrative: a piece of writing or speech that tells a story.

Narrator: the 'voice' or character that tells the story. Sometimes the narrator may be the writer but sometimes it may be a character created by the writer. The narrator may tell the story from a first-person perspective, using the words 'I', 'my', and 'we' or he or she might tell it from a third-person perspective, using 'he', 'she', 'his', 'her' and 'they'.

Onomatopoeia: the use of words whose sounds copy the sounds of the thing or process they describe. On a simple level, words like *bang, hiss* and *splash* are onomatopoeic.

Oxymoron: a figure of speech which puts together words of opposite meaning, e.g. *bitter sweet.*

Parody: a kind of writing that copies the style of another writer or style of writing, often with the purpose of making fun of the original.

Pathos: an effect in writing that makes the reader feel sadness or pity.

Plot: the main storyline, e.g. of a novel or play.

Pun: a play on words that often have a similar sound but different meanings in order to create a humorous effect.

Purpose: the reason behind a piece of writing or why a speech has been made, e.g. to entertain, to explain, to persuade, to argue.

Prose: Any text that is not written in verse. Prose includes things like novels, non-fiction texts and biographies but does not include poetry and some drama.

Rhyme scheme: the pattern of rhymes in a poem.

Simile: a comparison of one thing to another in order to make description more vivid. Similes use the words *like* or *as* to make the comparison, e.g. *The ice was like glass under foot.*

Stage directions: Instructions included in drama texts, explaining how scenes should be acted, what characters should be doing or even what the set and the costumes should look like.

Slang: distinctive words and phrases associated with informal speech. Very often it is used within certain social groups or age groups.

Soliloquy: a speech given by a character alone on stage or at least out of earshot of other characters, in which the speaker expresses his or her feelings to the audience.

Sonnet: a fourteen-line poem, usually with ten syllables in each line.

Stanzas: the groups of lines into which a poem is divided (the correct term for what are sometimes called 'verses').

Structure: the way that a poem, play or other piece of writing has been put together. This can include the metre pattern, stanza arrangement and the way ideas are structured and developed.

Symbol: like images, symbols are things which represent or indicate something else, e.g. a red rose can symbolize love, or the colour blue can symbolize purity.

Synonym: different words with the same or similar meanings, e.g. *shut* and *close* or *ship* and *vessel*.

Syntax: the way sentences are structured.

Theme: a central idea or message that a writer explores through a text.

Tone: the tone of a text is created through the combined effects of a number of features, such as vocabulary, syntax and rhythm. The tone can be a major factor in establishing the overall impression of a piece of writing.

Vocabulary: the words of a language.

OXFORD
UNIVERSITY PRESS

Oxford University Press is a department of the University of Oxford. It furthers the University's objective of excellence in research, scholarship, and education by publishing worldwide in

Oxford New York

Auckland Cape Town Dar es Salaam Hong Kong Karachi
Kuala Lumpur Madrid Melbourne Mexico City Nairobi
New Delhi Shanghai Taipei Toronto

With offices in

Argentina Austria Brazil Chile Czech Republic France Greece
Guatemala Hungary Italy Japan South Korea Poland Portugal Singapore
Switzerland Thailand Turkey Ukraine Vietnam

Oxford is a registered trade mark of Oxford University Press in the UK and in certain other countries

© Oxford University Press 2011

The moral rights of the author have been asserted.

Database right Oxford University Press (maker)

First published 2011

All rights reserved. No part of this publication may be reproduced, stored in a retrieval system, or transmitted in any form or by any means, without the prior permission in writing of Oxford University Press, or as expressly permitted by law, or under terms agreed with the appropriate reprographics rights organization. Enquiries concerning reproduction outside the scope of the above should be sent to the Rights Department, Oxford University Press, at the address above.

You must not circulate this book in any other binding or cover and you must impose this same condition on any acquirer

Third party website addresses referred to in this publication are provided by Oxford University Press in good faith and for information only and Oxford University Press disclaims any responsibility for the material contained therein.

British Library Cataloguing in Publication Data
Data available

ISBN: 978-0-19-913888-3

10 9 8 7 6 5 4 3 2 1

Printed in Great Britain by Ashford Colour Press Ltd., Gosport.

Acknowledgements

The author and publisher are grateful for permission to reprint the following copyright material:

Roddy Doyle: extract from *Paddy Clarke Ha Ha Ha* (Minerva, 1994), copyright © Roddy Doyle 1993, reprinted by permission of The Random House Group Ltd. **Harper Lee:** extract from *To Kill a Mockingbird* (Wm Heinemann 1960/ Vintage 2004), reprinted by permission of The Random House Group Ltd. **Owen Sheers:** 'The Farrier' from *Skirrid Hill* (Seren, 2005), copyright © Owen Sheers 2005, reprinted by permission of the author c/o Rogers, Coleridge & White Ltd, 20 Powis Mews, London W11 1JN. **John Steinbeck:** extract from *Of Mice and Men* (Penguin, 2006), copyright © John Steinbeck 1937, 1965, reprinted by permission of Penguin Books Ltd. **Herbert Williams:** 'Jones the Grocer' from *Wrestling in Mud* (Cinnamon Press, 2007), reprinted by permission of the author.

Illustrations by Q2A.